To Jack,
With

Sheila Extraurs ...

CW00409771

Swearing Like
a Trooper

Swearing Like a Trooper

M. J. Trow

Constable • London

Constable & Robinson Ltd
55-56 Russell Square
London WC1B 4HP
www.constablerobinson.com

First published in the UK by Constable,
an imprint of Constable & Robinson Ltd, 2013

A copy of the British Library Cataloguing in Publication
Data is available from the British Library

ISBN 978-1-47210-982-8 (hardback)
ISBN 978-1-47210-983-5 (ebook)

Printed and bound in the UK

1 3 5 7 9 10 8 6 4 2

Contents

1 In the Beginning

Maintain your rank, vulgarity despise;
To swear is neither brave, polite nor wise.

CHILLICOTHE ASSOCIATION FOR PROMOTING MORALITY
AND GOOD ORDER, *ADDRESSES OF THE CHILLICOTHE ASSOCIATION*
(JOHN ANDREWS, CHILLICOTHE, 1815)

In the past, in a solemn situation, men took an oath. Christians took it on the Bible, Muslims on the Koran, Jews the Talmud. Whatever their faith, these men were promising to tell the truth to those who heard them and, above all, to their God. In British courts today, we still say, 'I swear by Almighty God that the evidence I shall give shall be the truth, the whole truth and nothing but the truth.' A man's word was his bond; it was one of the cornerstones on which society depended.

We have to get to the fifth definition of the word 'swear' in the *Oxford English Dictionary* to find the meaning we want – 'Use a profane or indecent word or phrase in anger or as an expletive; use such language habitually.' But it is not difficult to see how one

1

definition led to the other. 'Swear not at all,' warned St Matthew, 'neither by heaven, for it is God's throne. Nor by the earth, for it is his footstool.' Quakers in the seventeenth century took him literally and no bad language passed their lips at all. How they coped when they stubbed their toes can only be imagined. Yet the same part of the Bible almost uses the word in the same way that we mean it: 'Then he began to curse and to swear, saying, I know not the man.' So Peter helped sell Jesus down the river.

We are not so much concerned in this book with profanity with a religious connotation.[1] We are concerned with the ribald slang of the Second World War, which in terms of casualties, civilian as well as military, was the bloodiest in history. The six years of fighting remain unique. The war has become known as the People's War because civvy street itself was the front line. Earlier on, wars were on a much smaller scale and only civilians who lived in the war zone were directly involved in the fighting. One of my wife's favourite cartoons from the sadly now-defunct satirical magazine *Punch* has a medieval husband struggling into his tights and saying to his still sleepy wife in the bed behind him, 'Something's bothering the sheep down in Bosworth Field.' If you were a civilian living in Bosworth Field

---

[1] Melissa Mohr cleverly breaks up the two broad types of bad language in her book *Holy Sh*t* (Oxford University Press, New York, 2013). In our context, the 'Shit' is more to the fore than the 'Holy'. And please note that even in 2013, 'Shit' has to have an asterisk in it!

(actually Ambien Hill over Dadlington Way) in 1485, you were likely to be in the thick of it. If not, you would barely know there was a war on at all.

The Second World War wasn't like that. Because of the wireless, widespread literacy and thousands of tons of high explosives coming down from the sky, *everybody* knew about it. The experiences of the men, women and children who lived through this war (and many who did not) were firsts and they responded in different ways. One of these ways was an explosion of swearing, as though somebody had opened the floodgates.

Three centuries earlier, Oliver Cromwell's New Model troopers in the Civil War of the 1640s had iron spikes driven through their tongues for blasphemy; God was not mocked. Nobody turned a hair if, 300 years later, one of Bernard Montgomery's Eighth Army let rip. Times, like the language, have changed. Or have they . . . ?

There was one gesture common to the Second World War and the Hundred Years War (1337–1453)[2] – the twin fingers of derision. The English archers who beat the French at Crécy, Poitiers and Agincourt waved their fingers to show the enemy they still had their secret weapon – the longbow – and the ability to use it. In 1940, Winston Churchill, the new Prime Minister, made the 'V for Victory' sign his own. It caught on – even the Germans used it!

---

[2] Yes, I know the dates don't add up, but calling it the Hundred and Sixteen Years War is a bit lame, somehow.

Universal soldiers

But before we go on, perhaps we should discuss why we swear at all. Dr Timothy Jay of the Massachusetts College of Liberal Arts explains: 'The point of swearing in many cases is to vent one's emotions and convey emotional information about one's state of mind to others. No other language is this efficient or effective . . .'

Given that war is *the* human activity likely to cause most emotion in the people fighting it, it is not surprising that the Second World War saw a swearing explosion on all fronts, both literal and metaphorical. Incidentally, Timothy Jay has noted that children start swearing between the ages of three and four. Did the tots of the Second World War, surrounded by adults 'effing and blinding', therefore become the swearing delinquents of the 1950s, the Cosh and Teddy Boys who seemed at the time to be the end of civilization as the older generation knew it?

Professor Jean-Marc Dewaele of Birkbeck College, University of London, takes us directly into war when he says swearing 'allows us to let off steam in a more or less acceptable way. It's better to swear than to hit . . . somebody in anger.' In the Second World War, of course, men did both. 'It can,' he goes on, 'give us extra energy to endure pain.'

This has actually been tested. It is called stress-induced analgesia and is linked to the flight-or-fight mechanism triggered by swearing, which we know is likely to cause offence to some people. Dr Richard Stephens of Keele University has proved that people can hold their hands for longer in ice-cold water if they swear than if they don't. I wonder if the men of the Arctic convoys used this technique, ploughing through ice-bound seas in the 1940s at temperatures as low as −60°C, temperatures, which would remove the skin and flesh from the hands of anyone foolish enough to touch bare metal. If, like me, you've taken a school party over one of those gallant ships moored in the Thames, HMS *Belfast*, in a miserable, cold January, you might be tempted, as was I, to let rip a little (not in front of the children, of course).

Peter Foot, currently chairman of the National Campaign for Courtesy, makes the point that most people swear in company when they feel comfortable. So the camaraderie of the Second World War, found in civilian life as well as in the Forces, was a natural breeding ground for this. We were all in it together; we had to pull in our belts, make do and mend, keep Mum, dig for England; all the time remembering that careless talk 'costs lives'. This communal spirit is something that disappeared after VJ Day (see Chapter 6) but it is one of the experiences people remembered most.

Most scientists today believe that swear words originate in the limbic system, the instinctive lower part of our brains, which matches what polite society has always believed, that swearing is a revolting habit of the lower orders (see Myth 1). Polite people, driven to exasperation over some incident or problem, would use the alternative 'dash' for 'damn' and 'Gad' for 'God'. There may have been a war on, but there were standards.

Myth 1
Only Thick Knarres Swear

One of the alternative 'swear like a . . .' phrases includes the phrase 'swear like a lord' (1531). Since the phrase 'drunk as a lord' seems to have been current too, it doesn't perhaps say much for the upper classes' behaviour in general. The idea is that the aristocracy and, below them, the gentry, could say what they liked because they were loaded. Stupid people (aka Geoffrey Chaucer's thick 'knarres'[3] in the 1380s) on the other hand, did not have much of a vocabulary, so they were forced back on foul-mouthed slang. This is just not true, but it was the current thinking in the Second World War. So officers did not swear, but other ranks did. And if you believe that . . .

Edwin Battistella explains in his book *Bad Language*: 'Vulgarity and obscenity refer to words or expressions which characterize sex-differentiating anatomy or sexual and excretory functions in a crude way . . . with the distinction between vulgarity and obscenity being primarily a matter of degree and prurience.'

OK? Got it? No? Never mind. Keep calm and read on.

---

[3] The word means a sturdy oaf, with the emphasis on the wooden-headed and none too bright.

So, what about the title of this book – *Swearing Like a Trooper*? Technically, a trooper was a cavalry soldier (although, as horsed warriors, they had virtually disappeared from the battlefield by 1939). Most of the horsed cavalry regiments became mechanized during the 1930s because the development of long-range artillery and the tank in the First World War made them obsolete. Horses *were* used in the Second World War but not for the dash and fire of the heroic cavalry charge – that would have been suicide. Were the cavalry more likely to swear than any other branch of the forces – say the infantry or the Navy or the RAF? It is all part of the image of the 'brutal and licentious soldiery' (Rudyard Kipling, *Life's Handicap*, 1891). Traditionally, as Wellington said, soldiers were 'the scum of the earth and sweepings of the gaols' (although he added that the British Army had made men of them). Among such people, swearing was a way of life.

The soldiers of 1939–45 were a very different breed. There were regulars, career-soldiers who had chosen the Forces voluntarily (even if some of these had only put on a uniform to escape the Depression of the 1930s); but most men were drafted in under the National Service (Armed Forces) Act of 3 September 1939 (conscription of all men aged eighteen to forty-one) and as such they came from all walks of life and every social class. They even included women!

And troopers were not the first group to be accused of bad language. Randle Cotgrave's dictionary of 1611 has the phrases 'swears like a carter' and 'swears like an abbot'. John Webster in *The White Devil* (1612) points an accusatory finger at falconers; Peter Motteux, translating Rabelais in 1693, thought tinkers were a pretty rough lot. In fact, not giving a tinker's damn survived into the war years we are talking about.

The first mention of the phrase 'swear like a trooper' is by the anonymous author of *The Devil to Pay at St James's* in 1727 and the phrase has stuck ever since.

Still keeping calm and reading on? Good. However, if you are easily offended by expletives, please do not read on. If, on yet another hand, you want to know the kind of language our parents, grandparents and great-grandparents were using in the People's War between 1939 and 1945, have yourselves a testicle. (I can't put it more politely than that!)

2 'The Day Swore Broke Out, My Missus Swore at Me . . .'[1]

Prime Minister Neville Chamberlain did not use a single expletive in his broadcast to the nation on 3 September 1939. It is a safe bet, however, that quite a few of those listening intently to their wireless sets did, even though it was a Sunday. History has been a little unkind to Chamberlain. Famously duped by Hitler (but then, who wasn't?) at Munich in 1938, the Prime Minister assumed that the Führer had a streak of morality and commonsense – he had neither. Throughout the 1930s Germany set about undoing what it considered to be the unfair Treaty of Versailles, building up its armed

---

[1] With apologies to the wartime comedian Rob Wilton. His tag line was actually, 'The day war broke out, my missus said to me . . .'

forces and marching into countries that didn't belong to it on the grounds that they needed *'lebensraum'* (living space).

No book on swearing can just jump in on a given date, as it were, with a blank page. The men, women and children who heard Chamberlain had fathers, brothers and even sons who had fought the 'Great War for Civilization' (1914–18) and at least some of their swearing must have come from them. They in turn, of course, picked it up from the previous generation and so on. Shakespeare's famous 'Seven Ages of Man' from *As You Like It* has a soldier 'full of strange oaths and bearded like the pard.'[2] We have to start somewhere nearer to our own time, so 1914–18 is as good a place as any. It was supposedly the 'war to end wars' but things didn't work out quite like that. Let me just throw in a word of caution from an earlier war.

On 25 October 1854, 678[3] men of the Light Cavalry Brigade of the British Army charged the gun emplacements of the Russian Army because of a misinterpreted order. There is little doubt that members of that infamous charge did indeed swear like troopers that day as they were 'stormed at with shot and shell' (Alfred, Lord Tennyson, the Poet Laureate, was much more polite about it). In the front line were the 17th Lancers and at one point Private Thomas Dudley shouted to

---

[2] A 'pard', by the way, is a lion, not a leopard. Technically, the three lions on the English shield (yes, all right, and the modern football shirt) are leopards in heraldic terms.

[3] The actual number is in dispute.

his friend Peter Marsh riding alongside him, 'Did you notice what a hole that bloody shell made?' Marsh was not amused:, 'Hold your foul-mouthed tongue,' he shouted back. 'Swearing like a blackguard when you might be knocked into eternity next minute.'[4]

Fast forward eighty-nine years. In 1943, Lieutenant John Randall joined the 1st SAS and was introduced to his colonel, the legendary Paddy Mayne, Irish rugby international and winner of four Distinguished Service Orders. With his hot temper, his Irish background, his rugger-hearty reputation, you might think that Mayne was the very model of a wartime swearer, but you would be wrong. The Colonel tolerated no insulting references to women in the Mess and no bad language. Even to use an innocent phrase like 'bloody fool' would lead to Mayne's idea of discipline – a right hook that would land the swearer flat on his back.[5]

---

[4] Quoted in John Harris, *The Gallant Six Hundred*. It's all relative, of course – 'blackguard' itself was pretty heavy stuff in 1854.

[5] Interview with John Randall, February 2013.

Dreaded *** and -------

The moral of these two stories is that gauging the level of swearing at any given time is surprisingly difficult. If you turn to print, you will find that no book and no newspaper printed in wartime Britain carried even the mildest expletive.[6] Instead, asterisks or straight lines replaced the offensive word or phrase. What about the wireless which was a godsend in terms of propaganda and keeping ordinary people abreast of what was happening? Nothing there either; the BBC had only just stopped having its announcers wear evening dress and you would get nothing other than perfect English and perfect decorum from someone like newsreader and announcer Alvar Lidell. So we have to turn to the man in the street – the one lined with sandbags by 1940 and where they'd taken away the street name – to see what swear words he used. And that, too, is fraught with difficulty. Historically, swearing is part of a male-dominated, macho culture, so a firewatcher, policeman, ambulance driver, soldier, sailor or airman might well use language in his workplace he would never use at home.

---

[6] But see the *Daily Mirror* after Dunkirk (Chapter 6).

Blankety-Blank

According to the *Philadelphia Evening Public Ledger*, a secretary at an American YMCA centre on the Western Front in 1918 wrote:

Cigarettes were blanket-blank cigarettes. Chocolate was blanket-blank-blank chocolate. They [the troops] were in a blanket-blank hurry. It was a blanket-blank long and blanket-blank hot blanket-blank march to their blanket-blank destination . . . I told them I was no preacher, but I said this war was going to be over pretty soon and they'd be going back home. 'When you get back,' I said, 'you'll sit down at the family breakfast table . . . and you'll reach across . . . and say "Godammit, Ma, where in hell's the butter?"' Those fellows stared at me when I got through and didn't laugh and one of them said, 'Why, dammittohell, you're right!'

The face that launched a thousand ships. Lord Kitchener made some appalling decisions in the First World War, particularly at Gallipoli. As Margot Asquith apparently said (although she herself attributes the remark to her daughter), 'He was not a great man but at least he was a great poster.' A lot of people swore when mentioning his name.

J. B. Priestley noted there were three kinds of England in the late 1930s. One was the Old England of castles and cottages, leafy lanes and a pace of life that seemed unchanged for centuries. It was here you could hear a local describe girls staring through a camp fence at the Americans, over here by 1942, that they were all 'prick-mazed'. There was the England of coal and steel, pottery, cotton and wool in which you might overhear a man ask. 'Oo's the bloody shit 'oo invented this way o' doin' up a fuckin' overcoat?' And there was the New England of hiking, the wireless, huge dance halls and Woolworths; this was urban England where perhaps the new swearing of the 1940s would catch on quickest.

So what did the men and women of the People's War of 1939–45 get from those of the Great War of 1914–18 in terms of bad language? Let's look at the Tommies' marching songs first. Virtually all of these were new words to old tunes. Some of them were music hall, some were hymns and the men in the trenches were familiar with both. 'Fred Karno's Army', sung to the tune of 'The Church's One Foundation' ('Aurelia') asks what bleedin' use those soldiers are. 'Après la Guerre', sung to Sous les Ponts de Paris', is very twee – 'Mademoiselle in the family way' is an example of the 'Franglais' used and the idea is as old as the hills, not likely to cause offence to anyone. After the war is over, 'Mademoiselle can go to hell', pregnant though she may be. 'She Married a Man' has survived as a rugger song – 'But she married a man who had no balls at all, No balls at all, No balls at all . . .' 'Tiddlywinks,

Old Man', sung to 'Hornpipe', ends with 'You'll never get your bollocks in a corned beef can' and the previous five lines are completely innocuous. Even so, at the time, usually only the first line was sung and the rest of the tune was whistled.

There didn't seem to be much sense or awareness of anatomy in some songs. 'Barney' takes his girl for a ramble but she trips 'and arse over bollocks she came'. Then again, there was the Tommies' version of 'John Brown's Body' – 'John Brown's baby's got a pimple on his – shush!' and in case you missed it, the line is repeated twice more. If you don't understand it, the last line thunders 'The poor kid can't sit down.' Get it?

Probably the best-known song of the First World War is 'Mademoiselle from Armentières', the key line of which runs 'Mademoiselle from Armentières, She hasn't been — for forty years, Inky-pinky-parley-vous.' The missing expletive (the dreaded straight line as it is printed in books of the period) is taken from a version of the song in the *Daily Telegraph Dictionary of Tommies' Songs and Slang* compiled in 1930 by two men who had fought in the trenches. Some habits die hard and they simply could not print the missing word (shagged or fucked would fit the rhythm). The authors admit that 'propriety has suppressed one or two of the songs and amended a few others'. Which underlines our difficulty.

The hymn 'What a Friend We Have in Jesus' had a superb soldiers' version called 'When This Blasted War Is Over'. An alternative is 'Lousy War' but it was the last line of the first verse that polite society would have been horrified by: 'I shall tell the Sergeant-Major to stick his passes up his arse.' You just don't talk to Sergeant-Majors like that.

Recruitment and Fornication

The Passing Show of 1914 was a popular revue performed at the London Hippodrome as an aid to recruiting (there was no conscription until 1916) and carried a number called 'On Sunday I Walk Out with a Soldier'. If you've seen the incomparable film *Oh! What a Lovely War* you'll remember Maggie Smith singing this one and the two drunks on home leave wondering how they can fill their time – 'Let's go to my Auntie Flo's place.' The trench version has:

> I don't want a bayonet up my arse-hole,
> I don't want my bollocks shot away,
> I'd rather stay in England,
> In merry, merry England,
> And fornicate my bleeding life away.

'Fornicate' sounds terribly proper, but nothing else fits as well into the rhythm.

The problem with the use of swear words is to try to decide exactly when they were current and who said them. A soldier (or sailor or airman) is just a man in uniform who may well have sworn before he enlisted. *Specific* rude Army slang is surprisingly rare. So if we find the origin of the words of the songs above, we discover that 'bleeding' (which has no real meaning and does not come from 'bloody') was in use as early as 1857. 'The family way' appears in print for the first time in 1891. 'Go to hell' is nineteenth century although of course the idea of suffering in purgatory is as old as the Bible. 'Ball' is very old, but the doyen of slang compilers, Eric Partridge (1894–1979), does not list it at all without other words, e.g. 'open the ball', which obviously has a very different meaning. He does better with 'bollocks' (usually spelled 'ballocks' before 1940). It was standard English until about 1840 and then became a vulgarity.[7] 'Arse' was also perfectly acceptable until about 1700, but even in 1690 it appeared in print as 'ar—'.

---

[7] Why some words cease to be acceptable and others don't is one of those unfathomable problems lost in the mists of time. Sometimes people get round the problem by missing out letters to avoid giving offence. In that context 'I love you from the b-tt-m of my heart' sounds a little odd.

The F-word and Beyond

Whole books have been written today on the 'F-word'. The noun 'fuck', which Partridge describes as 'an act of sexual connection', dates from about 1800. Before that, the usual word was 'swive'. As a verb, fuck dates from the sixteenth century and probably comes from the Latin *pungere* meaning to strike (I personally can't hear much of a connection between 'pung' and 'fuck' but there you go). Many soldiers' terms for penis, which we will meet later, have weapon images, which is very appropriate in the present context. Incidentally, the wholly correct (and boring) word 'penis' does not appear in print until 1676 (at a time when both Charles II and Samuel Pepys were using theirs quite a lot, apparently). 'Shag', as an alternative, was very common in the trenches of the First World War and probably derives from 'shake'. It is eighteenth century and perhaps has something to do with the northern dialect word 'shake' meaning a prostitute. 'No great shakes' therefore might originally mean 'not very good in bed'.

The Empire Strikes Back

Some words that were still current on the outbreak of the Second World War came from the British Army's long association with the Empire. The East India Company had opened for business in the sub-continent as early as 1600 and British regiments were sent out there for years at a time. Sexual relationships, even marriages, happened regularly before 1857 when the Indian Mutiny changed all that. The once-cosy relationships broke down in a welter of accusation, counter-accusation and mistrust. 'Jig-a-jig' or 'zig-a-zig' (sexual intercourse) may come from India or perhaps from the Middle East where the Empire also extended.

The world maps that the Tommies of 1914–18 would have seen were covered in red, denoting the huge swathes of territory that still belonged to Britain. One of these was Egypt and here we find the word *'bint'* meaning a prostitute. The original Arabic was *'saida bint'* (good day, daughter) which was presumably the equivalent of the traditional Victorian 'Are you good natured, dearie?' used at home by prostitutes looking for trade. Wog, which has never satisfactorily been explained, was used to denote any native from anywhere the British Army or Navy would have been likely to have visited.

A lot of books will tell you that WOG means Westernized Oriental Gentleman, but experts doubt it.

Some contend that it comes from Golliwog, a black-faced doll made popular in the United States in the early years of the twentieth century – try buying one of those today!

The word did give rise to a whole family however:

Woggery – an Arab village
Wog bint – an Arab girl
Wog hut – an Arab hovel

Incidentally, Arab, by 1939, was often pronounced in the American way, 'Ayrab', which somehow makes it seem all the more unpleasant.

By 1939, various terms had crept into the language that were euphemisms for something altogether nastier. The Victorians had been past masters at this with legs (shock! horror!) becoming 'limbs' and breasts (pass the smelling salts!) 'baby's public house'. Many was the wartime old girl taking in some bedraggled East End waif under the evacuation scheme and using the word 'poppycock', blissfully unaware that it came from the Dutch *papa kak*, meaning 'soft shit'. Fuck and bugger had become effing and blinding by 1943 (see Chapter 4), but even those terms was usually used by men in male company. Incidentally, when writing his *Dictionary of Forces' Slang* in 1948, Eric Partridge and his collabora-tors habitually substituted the word 'muck' for 'fuck'. I really find the 'm' word offensive – especially when they tell us the well-worn phrase was 'Muck you, I'm all right!' It's difficult, from this vantage point, to know what all the muss was about.

Johnny Foreigner

Racist and xenophobic slurs, which today are often regarded as the worst type of swearing, already existed in 1939. Frog for Frenchman dates from 1750; Yid for Jew a hundred years later. Hun, Boche, Fritz, Jerry and Kraut, all pleasantries for Germans, were in use by 1919. An Italian was already a Wop or an Eyetie by then; a Nip was a Japanese person. We must not underestimate the seriousness of these words. A defendant in the Middlesex Police Court in 1915 gave evidence that 'he called me a German and other filthy names'. Incidentally, it was often the norm to blame swearing on another nation, just as the pox was attributed to foreigners.[8] This still survives today, when, after a particularly savage expletive, someone says, 'Excuse my French' (1895).

'Boche' came into use after the Franco-Prussian War of 1870–1 and it was a French term meaning a 'bad lot'. Many historians believe this was the first truly modern war. The French had one railway line to take troops to the front; the Prussians had twenty-six. No prizes for guessing who won there, then.

---

[8] We blamed the French for venereal disease; they blamed us. The Italians were guilty, so were the Spanish and Dutch. In fact, of course, we should all have blamed the Aztec king, Montezuma; sexually transmitted diseases, with the exception of AIDS, came from the New World.

'Hun' can be dated to 1914–18 after the destruction of Louvain, reminiscent of wholesale vandalism of the original Huns who attacked Rome. It may or may not have had to do with so-called 'Hunnish practices' (anal intercourse) which the Germans blamed on the Turks. They in turn pointed a finger at the Greeks.

'Jerry' was the most common term for Germans during the Second World War but the Americans preferred 'Kraut', which seems to have developed in Italy as the US troops moved north through the peninsula in 1944.

They also used the word 'Heinie' (a shortened form of Heinrich) whereas the British Guards regiments preferred 'Muller', after a common German surname.

'Eye-tie' (or Ity) was the most usual term for Italians (in the RAF it meant an Italian aircraft) but 'Wop' (originally a pre-war American term believed to stand for With Out Papers) caught on in all the services. This should not be confused with the W.Op, of course, who was a Wireless Operator in the RAF.

The poet A. P. Herbert wrote:

> Sock the Wops and knock their blocks;
> Sock the Wop until he crocks;
> Sock the Wop because he's mean;
> Wash the Wop – he isn't clean . . .

Once the Italians had overthrown Mussolini and joined the Allies, however, Herbert stopped calling them Wops at all.

Just before war broke out, one or two intellectuals were studying swearing. Robert Graves, himself a Great War veteran, wrote *Goodbye to All That* in 1929 and recalls, 'The greatest number of simultaneous charges that I ever heard brought against a soldier occurred in the case of Boy Jones, at Liverpool in 1917. They accused him, first, of using obscene language to the bandmaster. (The bandmaster, who was squeamish, reported it as "Sir, he called me a double effing c . . .").'

Graves and his fellow officers found the punishment for this 'heinous' crime – ten days' solitary and a spanking by the bandmaster (!) – very fitting. But Graves believed that swearing was actually in decline by the late 1930s. In 1936, he wrote, 'Of recent years . . . there has been a noticeable decline of swearing and foul language, and this . . . shows every sign of continuing indefinitely until a new shock to our national nervous system – envisageable as war . . . may (or may not) revive the habit, simultaneously with that of praying.'[9] Prophetic or what?

Graves's fellow memoirist of the Great War, Siegfried Sassoon, told an amusing story (which would have been much more amusing had his publishers not chickened out and used the dreaded straight line). Ormond, one of Sassoon's fellow officers, had a

---

[9] Robert Graves, Lars Porsena: *The Future of Swearing and Improper Language* (London, 1936). Like all public schoolboys of his generation, Graves would have learned some of the *Lays* (that's not a rude word) *of Ancient Rome* by Lord Macaulay, which began 'Lars Porsena of Clusium, by the nine gods he swore . . .'

portable wind-up gramophone on which he constantly played a hit song called 'Lots of Loving'. The others, including the Adjutant, pretended that the song contained an 'unprintable epithet'. Since the record was scratched that particular phrase was indistinct and everybody claimed to be annoyed that the record company actually produced such filth. Ormond was furious. 'I ask you,' he stormed, 'is it bloody likely that "His Master's Voice" would send out a record with the word -------- in it?'

Now, only God knows![10]

Robert Graves may have been right about swearing's decline although, allegedly, the last words of King George V, who died in 1936, were 'bugger Bognor'. This is almost certainly apocryphal. He actually said to a nurse giving him a sedative, 'God damn you.' Tut! Tut! Your Maj!

Shortly before the start of the Great War in defence of his use of the word 'bloody' on stage in *Pygmalion*, George Bernard Shaw maintained (in the *Daily News*, April 1914) that the word was 'in common use as an expletive by four-fifths of the English nation, including many highly-educated persons'.

---

[10] Robert Browning was once asked what one of his poems meant. He thought for a moment and then said, 'Once, Robert Browning and God knew what it meant. Now, only God knows.' A handy quote for all occasions.

Naughty Bits on the Eve of War

When it comes to sexuality in swearing on the eve of the Second World War we are in a strange twilight world. Women had only gained the vote in 1928 and although they had done stalwart work in the munitions factories of the Great War, nobody accepted them as men's equals. Women who smoked in public and went into pubs unescorted were still frowned upon. Polite society used the term 'no better than she should be' and raised the eyebrow of disapproval. 'Bird', 'tart', 'vamp' and 'tramp' were used, too, and *'femme fatale'* had an exotic foreign sound to it. English ladies didn't behave like that.

Homosexuality was even murkier; underground because it had to be. Sexual acts between men were made illegal in 1884 so 'queen', 'homo', 'pansy', 'queer' and 'nancy boy' were all prevalent in 1939 although the topic was largely ignored.

The only well-known homosexual between the wars was Quentin Crisp, one of the self-styled 'Stately Homos of England'.

This was the state of swearing play in September 1939, but it was all about to change. The famous collector of slang, Eric Partridge, said, 'War is the greatest excitant of vocabulary', and American writer J. L. Dillard claimed, 'The big watershed insofar as explicit terminology was concerned was probably World War II.'

Myth Two
Hess[11] Is a Four-letter Word

Many books that want to avoid bad language will tell you that single-syllable 'naughties' were brought over by the Anglo-Saxons. This simply isn't true. Admittedly, we can only measure first-usages by the written word but that, presumably, post-dates the usages of such words in everyday speech.

So 'shit' appears by AD 1000, as does 'arse'. 'Turd' is there too, so technically we only have three Anglo-Saxon terms. 'Cunt' appears *c.*1203 (I bet it was aimed at King John!), 'fart' in 1250, 'piss' forty years later, 'cock' *c.*1400 and, the most famous of all, 'fuck' not until *c.*1503. (Note that the snobby Normans didn't use any of these in the Domesday Book in 1087). And on that note, I wonder if the thirteenth-century residents were embarrassed to give their address as Gropecunt Lane.

When William Langland wrote *Piers Plowman* (sometime between 1360 and 1387), writing tweely about Heaven, he avoided such words, but Geoffrey Chaucer in *The Canterbury Tales* (1386) sprinkles 'farts' and 'queyntes' all over the place, especially in 'The Miller's Tale'.

---

[11] Rudolph Hess was Hitler's deputy. He flew to Scotland in May 1941 to broker a peace deal but was probably lured by British Intelligence.

All four-letter words quoted above (except perhaps Hess!) would have been known to millions of Englishmen (and quite a few women) by 1939. The problem is trying to decide how many of them actually said them in public.

What was going on between 1939 and 1945 that made it more acceptable to swear than ever before? Molly Lefebure was a young journalist who got one of the most fascinating – and unlikely – jobs in the country in 1941 when she became secretary to Cedric Keith Simpson, the Home Office pathologist. Traipsing around behind the great man from murder scene to murder scene and in and out of mortuaries, she saw some pretty unpleasant sights. But she was also a great observer of human nature:

> I think the main reason for the success of the British
> was that they enjoyed the war . . . It gave them all the
> chance to do all the daring things they have excelled
> at throughout their long history and a lot of new,
> twentieth century daring things into the bargain . . .
> For six glorious years they were able to be soldiers,
> sailors, airmen, guerrillas, frogmen, spies, bomb
> experts, nurses, rescue workers, ambulance drivers,
> explorers, plotters, schemers, saboteurs . . .

And, she might have added, it gave them the chance to swear.

But there was more to it than that. Molly Lefebure talks about war-weariness, which is almost the flipside of her views above:

> Some it made drink a lot. Others took to bed –
> with others – a lot. Some became hideously gay,[12]
> brave and hearty. Others became sardonic and bored.
> Some curiously depressed. The Cockneys sharpened
> their celebrated wit until it had an edge which cut as
> painfully and bitterly as grass.

Simpson, Molly's boss, had his own comments to explain the 60 per cent increase in all types of crime during the war years:

> Emergency regulations, uniforms, drafting, service
> orders and a life of discipline cramp the freedom of
> many young men and during the long periods of
> wartime training and waiting, not a few of them got
> bored – 'browned off' was the common phrase – and
> got into trouble with local girls and camp followers

Simpson was concerned with more serious crimes than swearing – although people could be and occasionally were 'up before the beak' for doing that.

The bottom line is that the people of 1939–45 had a great deal to swear about. They were terrified of

---

[12] Happy, perhaps with a vague heterosexual connotation (in Victorian times, a 'gay lady' was a prostitute).

invasion, at least until 1942. At Dunkirk two years earlier, Hitler's Panzer divisions had been poised across the Channel and Operation Sea Lion was in place. All the Germans had to do was to knock out the RAF . . . Civilians were hit by bombs of all descriptions in the Blitz of 1940–42 when a new word – 'to coventrate' – entered the language to mean the devastation of a city, following the flattening of Coventry. The bombs returned in 1944–5 with the deadly unmanned V-1 and V-2 rockets, the Doodlebugs that brought back all the airborne terror of the earlier years. People's food and clothing were rationed. The austere Woolton pie was made of carrots; coupons only bought tiny amounts of butter, jam and meat. Chaps no longer had turn-ups on their trousers; girls painted seams up the backs of their legs with eyebrow pencils because sheer stockings had virtually disappeared.

Their children were sent away to the country for safety where undernourished townies discovered grass and cows and seasons for the first time. Everywhere was pitch-black at night and those few who had cars couldn't use them because petrol was at a premium. All over the country, an army of 'little Hitlers' sprang up, paid to pry and snoop by a paranoid government that was convinced there was a Fifth Column of spies operating in every street. 'Put that light out,' air raid wardens shouted. 'Don't you know there's a war on?' Desperate housewives, queuing for hours outside shops which sold almost nothing, would sidle up to the shopkeeper and whisper 'AUC?' (Anything Under the Counter?)

Were they down-hearted? Yes. And even that was a problem: defeatism was officially a crime by 1940.

Moriarty's Law

The sixth edition of *Moriarty's Law* was published in 1939; in theory every policeman in the country was supposed to have a copy and be familiar with its contents. There was no law against swearing in public *per se*, but it was implied in various sub-sections. For example, the Indecent Advertisements Act of 1889 meant that you couldn't write anything naughty on lavatory walls or stick obscene posters to trees, walls, fences, etc. You could not advertise a cure for VD (unless you were a Health Authority). You couldn't send dodgy material through the post or sell the stuff.

'Indecent language' was defined as 'unbecoming, not decent [!], contrary to propriety, or offensive to modesty'.

'Obscene' meant 'something disgusting, filthy, repulsive or offensive to chastity or delicacy'.

So you weren't allowed to be indecent, obscene or profane in the street, for example by singing a ballad, especially if you annoyed passers-by. No warrant was necessary for arrest.

In some places, local byelaws made it an offence to 'use any indecent language or gesture'.

For the record, the correct legal term for sodomy (anal intercourse) was 'buggery' and you got life for doing it.

So how bad was it? The following pages will tell all, but in the meantime, reflect on a case in June 1940. A defendant known only as 'Algernon' admitted to using an offensive word during an altercation outside a London tube station. The magistrate, Mr Broderick, asked what the expression was. 'Algernon timidly uttered Eliza Doolittle's adjective, the substantive being "swine". "Yes, I've heard that," said Mr Broderick, unmoved. He hears much worse language in the course of a week.'

3 'Bless 'Em All'

There's many an airman has blighted his life,
Thru' writing rude words on the wall ...
GEORGE FORMBY IN THE SONG 'BLESS 'EM ALL',
WRITTEN BY FRED GODFREY, 1917

There seemed to be no war at first. The infant television station run by the BBC at Alexandra Palace closed down; normal service was resumed six years later. There was the wail of air-raid sirens on that first day of the war, but it was a false alarm and a strange lull set in. We called it the 'phoney war'. The French, undergoing a similar experience, called it *drôle de guerre*. Even the Germans, who were already invading Poland, called it *Sitzkrieg* – the armchair war. The thousands of cardboard coffins stapled together in a panic to cope with the first wave of bombings went unused. The Luftwaffe had shown what this war would be like as early as 1937 when they had bombed the Spanish town of Guernica; but it didn't happen here. Not yet. All that was to come.

The British Armed Forces during the Second World War developed a clean slang of their own (although I'm not sure how genuine some of it was). It was based to an extent on the new weapons and technology that had been invented in the Great War and developed since then. We have a stereotypical view of such servicemen, partly through the heroic black-and-white war films of the 1950s.

The Strange Case of the Dog in the Wartime

On 17 May 1943, Guy Gibson led the famous Dambusters raid on the Mohne and Eder dams. The attack, by night, was extraordinarily difficult and made possible by the brilliant invention of bouncing bombs by Barnes Wallace and the courage of the RAF crews of 617 Squadron who flew the Lancasters. The casualties were high and Gibson won the Victoria Cross, later writing it all up in his *Enemy Coast Ahead* (which does not contain one naughty word).

The problem surrounding all this stems from the fact that Gibson had a black Labrador called Nigger (on account of his black coat). When they made the film *The Dambusters* in 1955 with Richard Todd as Gibson, sure enough, there was Nigger, joyfully wagging his tail on the tarmac. So far, so accurate. When I saw it on television recently, however, the 'N-word' had been blanked out.

The name Nigger was substituted with Trigger for the film's release in the US, which must have confused a lot of cinema-goers who believed that Trigger was Roy Rogers's horse (a palomino, not a black, thank God! – that would have confused them still more). Had the dog-actor ever found out about this, he would have been incensed – his name really *was* Nigger.

Now, a remake of the film is being planned with 'national treasure' Stephen Fry writing the screenplay. Apparently he has changed the dog's name to Digger.

The 'N' Word

Racial 'swearing' has taken over from sexual swearing in our own time, which is not only ludicrous but makes life very difficult for the rude-researcher of the Second World War, where such terms were widely considered to be jocular and not offensive at all. Nigger minstrels were cork-blacked singers of the Victorian music hall who still performed between the wars (and well beyond in the case of television's *Black and White Minstrel Show*). Nigger brown was an official colour, e.g. of wool and paint, and we've already seen it applied to RAF officers' dogs. So mundane was the word that the Navy used it in two contexts. Nigger spit was the hard lumps found in Demerara (brown) sugar; niggers in the snow were prunes and ground rice. When the terminally boring Sir John Anderson (he of the shelter) was burbling on in a House of Commons speech in 1940, a bored Labour MP shouted at him, 'Don't talk to us as though we were a lot of niggers.' Nobody turned a hair.

All in all, those who lived through the Second World War had a great deal more to worry about than whether the odd phrase gave offence. After all, we were all trying to kill each other and, conversely, to stay alive. The problem over the word arrived, predictably, with the Americans (see Chapter 5). The official advice from the British government was 'do not use the term nigger' (even though vast numbers of GIs did).

Officers were known as 'types'; other ranks as 'jobs'. The RAF officer types said things like 'Wizard prang' and 'Tally ho, Red Bandit Leader'. Naval officer types wore duffle coats, drank cocoa and were forever having conversations over the speaking tube – 'Bridge here, Number One'. Army officer types had all been to Sandhurst and were called 'Biffo'. To a man, they all had girlfriends called Celia and they lived in

Tunbridge Wells. In the films, of course, they were all played by Jack Hawkins or, if he wasn't available, David Niven.[1]

Other ranks were a more disparate lot, the raw recruits of any branch of the services usually portrayed in films by Richard Attenborough or Victor Maddern. But the horror story – of the Army in particular – was the Sergeant-Major (invariably William Hartnell) whose job it was to bully the conscripts into something resembling a fighting army. So detested was this figure that a new version of 'The Bells of St Mary's' was written about him:

> The balls of Sarn't Major are wrinkled and crinkled.
> Capacious and spacious as the dome of St Paul's.
> The crowds they do muster
> To gaze at the cluster;
> They stop and they stare
> At that glorious pair
> Of Sarn't Major's balls,
> Balls, balls, balls, balls.

---

[1] Niven was perhaps the most high-profile officer in a real-life and very elite unit, the GHQ Liaison Regiment, known as Phantom.

Myth 3
Hitler, He Only Had One Ball:
The Enemy's Anatomy

The most famous naughty slang song of the war has to be this one, sung to the tune of 'Colonel Bogey', but it's more complicated than you might think. The most common version is:

> Hitler has only got one ball,
> Göring has two but very small,
> Himmler is somewhat sim'lar,
> But poor old Goebbels has no balls at all.[2]

There are several slight variations on this version, e.g. 'Josef' instead of 'poor old' in the last line and Martin Bormann occasionally replaces the Reichsminister for Propaganda and Enlightenment completely.

Version 2 has:

> Hitler, he had but one left ball
> [Actually, we've *all* only got one *left* ball,

---

[2] We can officially correct the slur on Josef Goebbels. He had six children by his wife and possibly more with various mistresses. Presumably, therefore, he actually had a sufficiency in the testicular department. Hitler is more complicated. Following his suicide on 30 April 1945, his body was doused in petrol and set alight. Although post-mortems were carried out by the Soviets, they were loath to share any information with the West so the number of testicles the Führer possessed will forever be shrouded in mystery.

ladies excepted, of course]
Mussolini; he had none at all,
Stalin, he was three-ballin'
And that's the dictator's rise and fall!

Version 3 brings in regional variations:

Hitler has only got one ball,
The other is on the kitchen wall [or Albert Hall if
    you're a Londoner].
His mother, the dirty bugger,
Chopped it off when he was small.
She threw it into the apple tree [or over West
    Germany – a Cold War addition?]
The wind blew it into the deep blue sea,
Where the fishes got their dishes
And ate scallops and bollocks for tea.

Not to be outdone by the Albert Hall, Mancunians
substituted 'Free Trade Hall'; Loiners 'Leeds Town
Hall'; Glaswegians 'the Kelvin Hall'; Northern Irish
'the Ulster Hall'; and Liverpudlians 'St George's
Hall'. Outraged, Geordies had Frau Hitler throwing
her favourite son's testicle into the River Tyne.

Post-war Australian children sang:

Hitler had only one brass ball,
Ger-ring had two but they were small.
Himmler had something similar,
And poor old Go-balls had no balls at all.

Goballs often became Joe Balls, probably because Australia's kids didn't have much idea who Goebbels was. Australian troops had served in North Africa and Burma, so Field Marshal Rommel, the Desert Fox, was sometimes substituted in his place.

For reasons best known to themselves, the Boy Scouts of America substituted Ernie Röhm for Goebbels, even though Ernst Röhm, the leader of the *Sturm Abteiling* (brownshirts) was murdered five years before the war started.

As in the Great War, soldiers' versions of current hits never reached the airwaves, but unlike the Great War, servicemen and -women here and overseas had the opportunity to listen to the originals over the wireless and improvisation did the rest. The most famous must be a version of 'Bless 'Em All':

> Fuck 'em all! Fuck 'em all!
> The long and the short and the tall.
> Fuck all the sergeants and W.O.1s,[3]
> Fuck all the corporals and their bleeding sons.
> 'Cos we're saying goodbye to them all.
> As up the CO's arse they crawl,
> You'll get no promotion
> This side of the ocean.
> So cheer up, my lads, fuck 'em all.

---

[3] Warrant Officers, First Class.

By today's standards, of course, even the clean original versions might raise an eyebrow, but the racist and xenophobic slurs involved weren't considered slurs at all or they were used for propaganda purposes. There was, after all, a war on. Ronald Frankau wrote 'The Jap and the Wop and the Hun' and, when the Americans arrived, they sang 'We're Gonna Have to Slap That Dirty Little Jap' with great gusto. George Formby, he of the ukulele and goofy appearance, was rated by the Mass Observation[4] team as the biggest single morale booster of the war, ahead of Winston Churchill, the Prime Minister; Tommy Handley, the comedian; and Vera Lynn, the Forces' sweetheart. His Mr Wu was a stereotypical Chinese laundryman (Chinese restaurants had yet to make an impact in Britain) who was also an air raid warden:

> He goes around every night
> To make the blackout sure.
> So if you've got a chink in your window,
> Hey, you'll have another one at your door.

How we laughed!

---

[4] The Mass Observation unit was set up in 1937 by Tom Harrisson and Charles Madge as a socio-anthropological organization to study the habits, attitudes and opinions of the people. Once the war started, however, it came to be seen as a sinister snooping organization along the lines of George Orwell's Big Brother.

'Fornicating what, did you call me, De Gaulle?'
(with apologies to David Low, the great
Evening Standard cartoonist)

Incidentally, on the lines that foreigners were the cause of every problem known to man, the common overseas complaint called athlete's foot, which was a particular problem in jungle terrain, was known as Chinky toe-rot.

How Terribly, Terribly Vulgar –
The Naughty Bits of Noël Coward

On a *slightly* higher level, Noël Coward was writing topical lyrics for West End shows (Blitz permitting) and they reflect what was acceptable language for the stage and for mixed company. 'Imagine the Duchess's Feelings' appeared in 1941:

> Said the Duchess, 'Well!
> Something doesn't gel!'
> Said the Duchess, 'Well – Hell!'

Nothing shocking there. The women of the First World War had already allowed phrases like 'To Hell with the Kaiser' to be heard in mixed company. Coward provided more of the same with his famous 'Don't Let's Be Beastly to the Germans' in 1943:

> Let's help the dirty swine again –
> To occupy the Rhine again
> But don't let's be beastly to the Hun . . .
> . . . Let's soften their defeat again –
> And build their bloody fleet again.

Inexplicably, Churchill's paranoid government banned this song for a while, ignoring the obvious sarcasm of the sentiments and clinging literally to the title. They must have forgotten, temporarily, that Coward was working on and off as a secret agent – for the British, that is!

In 'I Wonder What Happened to Him' in 1944, Coward wrote:

He was stationed in Simla, or was it Bengal?
I know he got tight at a ball in Nepal
And wrote several four-letter words on the wall.
I wonder what happened to him!

The lyricist was poking fun at the old school of the Raj – still going, of course, until 1947 when the British pulled out of India, and the implication that an officer who writes on walls is a cad and a 'boundah' (see the opening verse of this chapter and the author's personal experience in Chapter 6).

Coward's 'Army Version' of 'Let's Fly Away' uses initials to disguise hard core swearing:

Let's fly away
Before we go completely 'daffy',
Where no one's ever heard of NAAFI[5]
And life is sweet F.A.

---

[5] The Navy, Army and Air Force Institute, responsible for Forces' food. The American term 'naff' derived from this and it meant 'Not Available For Fornication' in that the NAAFI looked after married quarters too.

'Sweet F.A.' was Fanny Adams, a little girl murdered and mutilated by a lunatic named Baker in Alton, Hampshire, in 1867. The term had become slang by 1900 and even, sickly enough, referred to tinned meat, but 'F.A.' to the soldiers, of course, was 'fuck all'. Did Noël Coward use it in that sense? Bearing in mind he was the first person to say (actually, sing) 'bloody' on the BBC, I wouldn't be at all surprised.

Incidentally, when I told you in Chapter 2 that no bad language was used on wartime wireless, I was clearly lying!

Fetch Out No Shroud for Johnny Under Ground

If the songs of the Second World War are not particularly helpful *vis-à-vis* swearing, what about its poetry? The poems themselves do not have the same impact as those of the First World War, with its trench horrors and the concept of 'lions led by donkeys', but they can give us a glimpse of the sort of bad language used and accepted. Interestingly, there is only one racist term that I can find and that is already in speechmarks, as though it's a little impolite even by 1941 when it was published. It is in A. S. J. Tessimond's 'England' and one of the verses ends with the line, 'Smile at the "dirty nigger" cheated.'

Henry Reed, called up in that same year to join the Royal Army Ordnance Corps, just plain swore in 'Judging Distances'. Since Reed is complaining about authority's obsession with the trivia of tradition, usually called 'bullshit' in the Forces, his exasperation is entirely appropriate. When reporting artillery ranges you have to be as vague as possible. So if you see woolly creatures grazing in a particular field, you are not allowed to call them 'the bleeders *sheep*'.

John Pudney was a Squadron Leader in the Royal Air Force. In 'Combat Report' he wrote a line he would never have actually written to a distraught and grieving next of kin: 'He burnt out in the air: that's how the poor sod died.'

Jocelyn Brooke, of the Royal Army Medical

Corps, spoke of the boredom that long periods of any war are all about of soldiers waiting for something to happen and becoming bored with too much leisure – in fact, 'browned off with bints and boozing'.

Hamish Henderson, of the 51st Highland Division, imagined a conversation between a British Tommy and a dead German in 'Fort Capuzzo'– 'Cheerio, you poor bastard.' It implies a strange camaraderie of war between enemies that their respective governments would never have accepted or even understood.

Ex-student Gavin Ewart had joined the Royal Artillery by the time he went back to his alma mater in 'Oxford Leave' and met up again with a 'certain sort' some people chose to believe did not exist, 'a donnish type, a rather middle-aged queen'.

Staff officer Walter Andrewes makes a very telling point from the swearing point of view in 'Mess'. A captain had been telling his fellow officers just how grim a particular situation was in terms of casualties and human lives. This sort of conversation did nothing for morale and so the colonel stepped in and 'made things decent, with an indecent joke'.

The message is this. Swearing, certainly by 1945, had become widespread; so widespread, it was almost a relief to hear it, a sense that all was well. Most books on the subject will tell you that men swear most when they are in danger, but actually the reverse may be true. Most books too carry the story of the anonymous sergeant who would bawl at his unit away from the front, 'Get your fuckin' rifles.' But under actual attack, his order would be 'Get your rifles,' stressing the unfamiliarity and therefore the urgency of the situation.

Cockney Richard the Thirds

I'm always very dubious about cockney rhyming slang. Who has the time to make it up, especially when there's a war on? Even so, much of this was in common usage in the First World War and derives partly from thieves' cant of an earlier period, a method the underworld developed to disguise what they were up to. By 1939 it was so widespread that it gets lost in everyday language and most of it was clean, as in Rosie Lee for tea. The Army term anti-wank for anti-tank is one naughty example. So is family tree for lavatory. Contrived, or what?

Let's look at one of the most hyper-charged and dangerous situations in the Second World War: the landing on the Normandy beaches in June 1944 in the operation known as Overlord – D-Day. In just twenty minutes on Omaha Beach, the US Army lost 2,000 killed and wounded. Obviously, we can only go by the written record of the day and not all of those would have included the words for posterity they actually said and heard. Trooper Ken Tout of the 1st Northamptonshire Yeomanry heard an American serviceman criticizing the British Commander-in-Chief: 'Bloody beanpole Montgomery.' And a tank driver in Tout's own unit said to him, 'Bugger me if we're going to carry all that lot ashore.' In the case of Sergeant William Smith of the Intelligence Corps, fear and nature kicked in: 'In the silence after the fiftieth round one of us said he wanted a Jimmy Riddle.'

Bombardier Harry Hartill of the Royal Engineers was sure his captain wasn't bluffing when he 'drew his revolver and shouted "I'll shoot the first bastard that disobeys my orders".' T. Tateson was under accidental fire from his own side as the Green Howards moved off the Normandy beaches: 'and I sent the unauthorised message "Stop this fucking barrage".' It did stop, but Tateson realized that was the result of coincidence, not the shock among his comrades at reading his expletive.

So were there any swear words which can be linked directly to the Second World War? McConville and Shearlaw's *Slanguage of Sex* lists forty-two, although it is not always easy to differentiate between British and American. We will look at the impact of the Americans – GI Joe – in Chapter 5 but a word must be said here about other influences. The Free French, Poles and other nationalities based in wartime Britain obviously had swearing of their own,[6] but their numbers were too few to make much of a difference. Only the Australians had a colourful slanguage – Diggerese – that permeated through to the British and that was probably because we had fought alongside them before, first in Gallipoli in 1915 and later in the trenches of the Western Front.

The Great Australian Adjective[7]

The best known single word in Diggerese is 'bloody'. It preceded nearly every word spoken by an Aussie according to some sources. In 1915 the 'Australaise' was dedicated to the Australian Field Forces in Gallipoli. It was written by C. J. Dennis and sung to the tune of 'Onward Christian Soldiers':

Fellers of Australier,
Blokes an' coves an' coots,
Shift yer bloody arses ['carcases' in the original]
Move yer bloody boots.
Gird your bloody loins up,
Get your bloody gun,
See the bloody enermy

---

[6] *Le mot de Cambronne* (*Merde!*) – Shit! – was immortalized by Victor Hugo in *Les Misérables* and the name even became a euphemism – 'What a load of old Cambronne' – and even a verb '*cambronniser*' in French.

[7] A phrase coined in the *Sydney Bulletin*, August 1894, in what were politer days.

> An' watch the blighters run.
> Get a bloody move on,
> Have some bloody sense,
> Learn the bloody art of
> Self de-bloody-fence.
>
> But there was more to Diggerese than that. The Aussies had a reputation for plain-speaking. Here is a little list:
>
> Dinger (also Gonga) – anus
> Lot of cock – nonsense
> Not worth a cunt full of cold water – useless
> Pissaphone – urinal
> Pommie – British person (this was probably a pun on Tommy and almost always followed by 'bastard')
> Shiny arse – one who had a desk job at headquarters; a staff officer
> Upter (Uptershit) – complaint

In a variant of the comment by the YMCA secretary in Chapter 2, a famous joke concerns a returning soldier after the war who was asked by his family to tell them any jokes he had heard. He explained, rather red-faced, that the language was rather coarse 'out there' and he couldn't possibly repeat any of it. His family insisted, however, and said he could blank out any words he thought might offend them, so off he went: 'Blank

blank blankety blank, blank, blank, blank, blankety blank, fuck.'

Which brings us back to our age old problem of what happens to soldiers' swear words once said soldiers get into print. In 444 pages taken from his diaries, 'Weary' Dunlop only mentions one naughty phrase and that came from the mouth of a Japanese guard who used the phrase 'zig-a-zig' for intercourse. On the other hand, we know from other memoirs that British and Australian prisoners of war on the Burma Railway swore (at least under their breath) because most of their guards spoke virtually no English. Alistair Urquhart of the 51st Highland Division quotes a mate who muttered, 'Keep your head on, you Jap bastard; it'll be knocked off soon.'

Sergeant Albert Youngman was with the SAS in France in 1944 and became a prisoner of the Germans. They tied him to a wagon full of ammunition hoping to discourage the British from firing on it. Youngman's commanding officer was the non-swearing Paddy Mayne, who saw the truck but not the helpless bloke on top. Youngman remembered, 'I thought, "That's Paddy and we're in the shit!"' As it happened, Mayne's machine-gun fire missed and all was well. Colonel David Stirling, who had set up the SAS in the first place, was famously contemptuous of Army red tape and the high command, which he called 'fossilized shit'. Daubed on the wall of a troopship in 1941 was a phrase with a similar viewpoint, a variant of Churchill's famous reference about the RAF – 'the Few' – in the Spitfire summer of

1940: 'Never in the history of human endeavour have so few been buggered about by so many.'

Let's allow the last phrase in this chapter to be an entirely appropriate one. It has passed into legend and is attributed to almost anybody, but according to Paul Fussell in *Wartime: Understanding and Behaviour in the Second World War*, it was first uttered by an aircraftsman working on a Wellington bomber somewhere in Scotland. Clearly he was having serious technical problems when he said, 'The fucking fucker's fucked.' And everybody knew exactly what he meant.

Somewhere in Scotland . . .

4 The A–Z of British Forces Swearing

The following list is compiled from various sources and I have added a few comments where appropriate. The list is subdivided into four sections; one for each of the three armed forces and, to get us going, a generic one of words that were probably used by everybody in the services.

General

Absolute bastards – Military Policemen, recognizable by their red caps

All to cock – mixed up, confused. The usual state of things in the Forces

Ammunition – a sanitary towel or tampon. Based on the phrase 'Praise the Lord and pass the ammunition', attributed to two US navy chaplains during the attack on Pearl Harbor, 7 December 1941. It came into this usage because of the sense of relief in a woman who found she wasn't pregnant after all!

Anything on two legs (you'd fuck or shag) – male repartee concerning the discernment of sexual conquest

Arse about face – upside down, topsy-turvy

Arse-crawl – currying favour

Arsehole bored or punched – utterly at a loss

Arsehole to breakfast time – long, stressful period

Arse or elbow – total incompetence

As the actress said to the bishop – a bit like 'excuse my French' (see Chapter 2), it makes the actual sexual intention of a sentence harmless

Ballocking (or bollocking) – a jolly good telling off

Belly cousin – someone with whom you shared a woman. Servicemen overseas rarely visited brothels (e.g. Lavender Street in Singapore) on their own for fear of being robbed, so this idea of queuing and waiting their turn came naturally

Bitched – made a mess of. As in the Forces' variant of the *Pal Joey* song of 1940 in which 'bewitched, bothered and bewildered' becomes 'bitched, buggered and bewildered'

Bit of cuff/crumpet – a young lady, often, as they said in the 1930s, 'no better than she should be'

Blind – swear violently and colourfully, as in 'effing and blinding'

Bloodying – cursing or swearing. As the guru of slang, Eric Partridge, wrote, '"bloody", the universal expletive of our fathers, was almost entirely supplanted in the Second World War by another of sexual rather than sanguinary significance'. You see what we rude-researchers have to put up with?

Bolo – mad, incompetent

Bullshit – spit and polish, but adapted to mean 'rubbish'. The posh version – bovine excrement – did not exist in the Second World War

Bullshit baffles brains – the idea that sheer dogged perseverance will triumph over clever ideas any day

Bullshitter – usually an officer renowned for his insistence on smartness or someone who liked to impress with his superior knowledge (see Navy and Air Force variants)

Call girl – probably American but the term was used by British and Australian troops throughout the war. It derives from 'services' cards left in shop windows: 'For a good time, call . . .' The problems of having to go through the operator and pushing buttons A and B in wartime must have seriously cramped the style of some of these girls

Cherry – virginity, often used in the phrase 'to lose one's cherry'

Chew the bollocks off – deliver a severe reprimand

Cock – mate, pal, chum or 'nonsense' (for 'Poppycock', see Chapter 2)

Cock up – make a mess of

Crutch – sometimes spelt 'crotch'; 'Kick him in the crutch' was friendly advice offered in a fisticuffs situation

Dishonourable discharge – masturbation after an unsuccessful date. The original referred to a man who had been cashiered from the Forces for misconduct

DSO – Dick Shot Off. The Distinguished Service Order was an award given for gallantry and its slang variant dates from the Great War

DYFs – Damned Young Fools, a collective phrase for officers under thirty years of age (in an earlier war, French Marshal Lasalle had said, 'A Hussar who isn't dead by thirty is a blackguard')

Extract the urine from – take the piss out of; tease or ridicule

Family tree – lavatory (cockney rhyming slang)

Fanny – this one probably belongs to the Army but all Forces used it. In Britain, it meant vagina; in the United States, the buttocks. From that sense, it could mean hot air. The First Aid Nursing Yeomanry

(FANY) must have got awfully tired of hearing the same old jokes

FFI – Free From Infection. 'To have an FFI' was to undergo an inspection by the Medical Officer, especially in his endless search for VD (see VD)

Four-letter man – an unpleasant person (a shit, not to put too fine a point on it)

Frat – girlfriend. This phrase came from official sources, especially paperwork given to troops going overseas, not to fraternize with members of the opposite sex. Since the word comes from the Latin for brother, I have always found this quite confusing

French letter – contraceptive (the Americans called these, more sensibly, rubbers, but there was a chronic shortage of rubber once the Japanese had overrun Burma)

Frig – military operation, raid or battle. It implies boredom, waiting around for the action and the expectation that it is all going to go horribly wrong

Frigging – politer form of 'fucking', according to most slang compilations, but an anonymous sex-romp written by 'Walter' (c.1880) uses the word to mean masturbation

Fuck you, I'm all right – phrase always relating to somebody else's selfish attitude, never your own (see Navy and Air Force variants)

Gobshite – idiot, fool

Homework – a girlfriend, usually temporary

Inspection, short-arm – see FFI

Jacksie – anus

Jig-a-jig – sexual intercourse

Joe Soap or Joe Hunt (Cunt) – a no-hoper who was given all the worst jobs because he was too stupid to refuse

Latrine wireless/latrinogram – the gossip picked up when men were together at their morning ablutions, usually out of officers' earshot

Letch – leering at girls. This one is Victorian, but it assumed a new significance to any squaddie going ashore in foreign parts for the first time

Packet, catch or cop a – contract venereal disease

Passion wagon – a truck or lorry carrying servicemen on leave or to a place of entertainment. Civilian girls had them too to take them to Forces dances

Pig in shit – the height of comfort

Piss and wind – someone who talks nonsense

Piss-arse about – play the fool; waste time

Piss, go on the – take part in a bout of heavy drinking

Piss out of, take the – tease or pull one's leg

Piss-pocket – an untrustworthy person. It is worth remembering that, because of conscription, large numbers of thieves, pickpockets, frauds and career criminals of all types suddenly found themselves continuing their calling in the Forces

Poofter – loudly patterned civilian suit. The more modern meaning – homosexual – may have developed from an assumed unofficial 'uniform' worn by the 1950s gay community

Pro – prostitute. The most common variant and with the double inference of 'professional' as opposed to the enthusiastic amateurs lured by the uniform!

Puff – ladies' man. Comes from the sense of showing off and has no connection with 'poof' (see 'Poofter', above)

Pusher – a girlfriend, perhaps from the idea of women pushing prams

Raise a gallop – have an erection

Shaft – intercourse (from a male point of view). A slightly softer version of shag, in widespread use in the Great War

Shagged – exhausted. This was public-school slang from the nineteenth century, but presumably originated in the exhaustion resulting from energetic sex

Shit – heavy shelling or enemy gunfire

Shitehawk – an unpleasant outsider (but because of their sleeve flash of an eagle, this was also the nickname of the entire 4th Indian Division)

Shit-hot – very efficient

Shit or bust – do or die

Shit order – dirty or scruffy. There were a number of orders of dress in the Forces – full, mess, stable, walking out, etc.

Shit orderly – sanitary inspector

Shit-scared – frightened to death (or at least to the point of defecation)

Shitting bricks – terrified

Short and curlies – pubic hair

Short-arse – small man

Skirt patrol – walk with the objective of finding female companionship

SOBs – Silly Old Blighters/Bleeders/Buggers, the collective term for officers over thirty by officers under thirty (see DYFs)

Split-arse cap – the folding field service cap (often wrongly called a forage cap by civilians) as opposed to the peaked dress service cap

Square-pusher – girlfriend. Again, a reference to pushing a pram, this dates from the Victorian period of nursemaids 'walking out' with soldiers

Square-tack – girls

Subject normal – reversion to the usual topic of conversation in all the Forces, i.e. sex

Tiger piss – inferior beer bought in foreign parts (with abject apologies to the current manufacturers of Tiger Beer, an excellent brew which has no links to this item)

VD – venereal disease. Most Forces doctors used the term without bothering to identify the specific type. 'Weary' Dunlop, the famous Australian Army doctor who was a prisoner of the Japanese on the Burma Railway, says that the disease was virtually endemic out there

Army

Other ranks were known as Brownjobs, as opposed to officers who were Browntypes. According to Eric Partridge, the Army had the smallest number of new rude words but as it had the largest in the First World War, this is hardly surprising. 'It is the earthiest; it suffers no sea-changes, makes no stellar flights.'

Army form blank – toilet paper (one of the few Army forms that actually had a purpose)

Bazooka – penis. Probably American after the gun of the same name (a recoilless anti-tank weapon that came into use in 1942) which was used by all Allied Forces. This is typical of the male-organ-as-weapon metaphor

Berka – brothel. Named after Sharia el Berker, a notorious red-light district in Cairo which was out-of-bounds to British troops and consequently a magnet for most of them

Berthas – breasts, usually of the large variety. Named after a German anti-tank gun of the Second World War, but applied to heavy artillery in the Great War and earlier

Blue-pencil – euphemism for a swear word, e.g. 'That blue-pencil sergeant!' This refers to the censors' habit of obliterating letters home with a blue pencil for security reasons, thereby removing certain key words. In the American Forces, offensive or dangerous lines were physically cut out

Blue-veined steak – a descriptive term for an erection. Probably used in the British Army before 1939. The version 'trumpet' is more common in Scotland and the north of England

Bog man – low life, as in the four-letter man (see General section, above)

Brothel creepers – suede shoes, worn for example by the Long Range Desert Group in the Western Desert, 1941–2

Brown tongue – crawler; sycophant

Bunk up – intercourse. This dates from pre-war, but the numbers of bunks used of necessity in cramped barracks led to its widespread use

By the centre – a mild oath of disbelief, as in 'By crikey!' (i.e. Christ). Taken from the drill book of parade ground formations

By the left – as above. Oddly, there doesn't seem to have been a 'by the right', perhaps because it may have been confused with the standard English 'by rights'

Column of fuck-up – column of route. As with so many phrases like this, the assumption among the ordinary soldiers was that it would all end badly

Come the old soldier – to claim superiority because of experience. The response was 'Old soldier; old shit'

Cunt cap – field service cap (see 'Split-arse cap', General section)

Damn a horse! – cry of exasperation from an old soldier. This one must have been disappearing fast by 1939–45. It referred to the problems of transporting cavalry horses by ship; the animals often panicked and usually caused problems

Debollocker – land mine. Once trodden on, the metal fragments blew upwards, hitting the testicles en route

Drop a bollock/goolie – make a serious mistake

Drop your guts – break wind

Gooly chit – also known as a 'blood chit'. A chit was a written authorization that protected the bearer. It's a bit difficult to guarantee protection of one's testicles in this way, but thousands of servicemen lived in hope

Joe Erk – largely Canadian Army term for Joe Soap or Joe Cunt, a useless individual

PBI – Poor Bloody Infantry. Every section of the Forces felt itself the most put-upon and neglected, none more so than the foot-sloggers who looked with resentment at the flashier arms of the service

Poggled – very drunk

Pozzie – jam. This is hardly rude, but I include it here for the apocryphal First World War story of two soldiers having tea in a café: First soldier – 'Pass the bloody pozzie, Bill.' Second soldier – 'Hey, mate, remember where you are.' First soldier – 'Blimey! Sorry, mate; I meant, pass the bloody jam.'

Rupert – penis. One of the John Thomas, Dick and Percy stable of Christian names for male organs. Interestingly the term is in current Forces usage by other ranks for public-school officer types, probably with the same double meaning

Spade, go for a walk with a – defecate in the desert. The Eighth Army, first under General Wavell, then under Montgomery, fought Rommel's Afrika Korps there and a great deal of defecation went on

Spare wank – man with no specific job to do

Twillip – nasty or unpleasant person. Developed from 'twerp' and popular in the Guards' regiments

Wear the kilt – to be a passive partner in male gay sex. It may originally have been pre-war and derogatory among English regiments in reference to the Scots

Navy

Other ranks were Bluejobs, as opposed to officers who were Bluetypes. Partridge wrote, 'The Navy is the pawkiest, most Pepysian and cheeky of the three slangs; it is the most debonair; its laugh is a belly-laugh, its disgruntlements more rueful than bitter.' Samuel Pepys, by the way, not only used words like 'piss' in his famous diary of the seventeenth century; he was also Secretary to the Admiralty.

Arse of the ship – stern (the blunt end)

Arso – Armament Supply Officer

Bag shanty – brothel. Presumably this is part of the old warning: 'Never go singing with women'

Bird sanctuary – WRNS Headquarters in London

Blackouts – Wrens' regulation navy-blue knickers. These were the thick winter-wear variety (for younger readers, think Bridget Jones)

Bugger grips or gripsbuggers – side-whiskers of old

sailors. It was generally accepted that the Navy was the home of sodomy, so a pair of whiskers gave participants something to hold on to

Bull – too much ceremony was known as tiddley bull

Button your flap! – Shut up! A reference to bell-bottomed trousers or the neck flap of the traditional able seaman

Canary ward – the VD ward in a naval hospital, the walls of which were a bright yellow colour

Choke your luff! – Shut up! (The Navy seems to have specialized in this sort of order)

Dobash – girlfriend. 'It might be wiser,' wrote Eric Partridge, 'to refrain from an etymology.' Consider it done, me ol' slang compiler. Presumably, what Mr P is too shy to suggest is that 'dough-bashing' was similar to 'pud-pulling', i.e. masturbation

Dreadnought – condom. The original Dreadnoughts were top-of-the-range battleships in Edwardian England. By using a condom, presumably, there was nothing to dread; not pregnancy nor venereal disease

ETBs – Elastic Top and Bottom: Wrens' regulation knickers (see Blackouts)

Fanad – naval abbreviation for Fanny Adams (fuck all), see Chapter 3

Fearnought – see Dreadnought

Fishing Fleet – women who hung around the Ladies'

Lounge at the Union Club, Malta, on the lookout for eligible naval types

Floosie – prostitute. This one is always associated with the Navy, but it may originate in Flossie, a generic name for a prostitute in South Africa

Fuck you, Jack, I'm all right – the naval variation of the general term. Jack Tar, meaning a sailor, goes back to 1781 and Jack much earlier

Grable-bodied seaman – a boat crew's Wren. Named after the lusciously curved Betty Grable, the Hollywood pin-up

Heads – toilets for the ratings (officers defecated separately in the Round House) usually located starboard forrard (that's the right-hand side at the front to most of us)

Left hanging Judas – actually a rope left dangling over the side of a boat (after Judas Iscariot who, filled with remorse after selling Jesus out, hanged himself). It came to mean, during the war, a man whose girlfriend has stood him up or let him down

Naval engagement – sexual intercourse. Pun on 'navel'

Navy cake – rectum/anal intercourse. Traditionally, life on board ship was a hotbed of this because of the lack of females. 'Rum, sodomy and the lash' was Winston Churchill's summation of the Navy. And he should know – he *was* First Sea Lord!

Oh, Miss Weston! – this one could be general, but it started life in the Navy and was an expression of disapproval of strong language. Dame Agnes Weston was a philanthropist who wrote letters to sailors and set up homes for those down on their luck. She disapproved of their bad language and heavy drinking. So well known was she that when the frigate HMS *Supermare* was commissioned in 1940, the ship was known as Aggie on Horseback

Party – girlfriend

Piece of nice – very attractive girlfriend

Poor as piss – short of money or pathetic. Often followed by 'and twice as nasty'

Pump ship – urinate

Social tit (or poodle faker) – naval officer prone to paying polite calls on shore. Old school Navy

Up shit creek – 'without a paddle' usually follows. Lost or in a dangerous situation

Air Force

Known as the Brylcreem Boys, the 'new bug' of the Forces pinched words from the Army and Navy. Partridge wrote of the RAF, 'Because of its youth, it tends to be perky and occasionally a shade truculent.'

Air Commode – Air Commodore; presumably on the grounds that anyone with a rank as exalted as that had to be a shit

Arse-end Charlie – pilot in a Fighter Squadron who weaves backwards and forwards behind and above the rest of the unit to protect them from attacks from the rear

Arse-polishing – flying a desk somewhere relatively safe

Battledress – pyjamas. Used largely in the Sergeants' Mess with reference to tussles under the blanket; strenuous sex

Brown nose – sycophantic crawler (see Brown tongue in the Army section)

Bullshit morning – the weekly inspection by the commanding officer

Bumf – from bum fodder (toilet paper), leaflets dropped from the air (mostly for propaganda purposes). A bizarre instance of this was when thousands of leaflets were dropped along the River Kwai in Burma to tell railway prisoners 'You are now free men'

Earhole – arsehole

Fuck you; I'm fireproof – the RAF version of the civilian and Navy originals, again implying selfishness. The motto of the RAF was therefore unofficially changed to *Per Ardua Asbestos*

Gnat's piss – weak tea

Huffy – WAAF who plays hard to get by being cold and superior

IBA – Ignorant Bloody Aircrafthand

Kittens in a basket – WAAFs who are overfriendly with airmen. This one was used of WAAFs by other WAAFs, presumably the less-friendly ones who were likely to be Huffy

Midwaaf – pushy, interfering NCO of the Women's Auxiliary Air Force

Passion-killers – airwomen's service knickers. These garments were designed to be as unappealing as possible

Petal – effeminate homosexual

Piss-poor – terrible weather. Alone of the Armed Forces, the RAF's tactical ability was hampered by fog, low cloud and electrical storms

Pongo – derogatory term for an Army officer. All branches of the service were, of course, on the same side, but rivalry was intense and after a few beers, punch-ups were not uncommon

Shit – more appalling weather and there were elaborate

subdivisions of it: 'shit and derision' meant cloud with rain; 'shit and corruption' was cloud, rain and flak

Split-arse – daring or reckless bravery and there were a number of applications:

cap (cunt cap in the Army) – folding field service variety

landing – very chancy landing

merchant – test pilot or stunt pilot

turn – usually a skid as the aircraft hits the runway

Split-arsing about – carrying out dangerous manoeu-vres, usually low flying. The most celebrated victim of this was Douglas Bader, who lost both his legs in a plane crash in 1931 yet went on to fly with Fighter Command during the war

Squadron Bleeder – Squadron Leader (*usually* affectionate)

Target for tonight – girlfriend. This one comes from the orders given to Bomber Command pilots in their briefings for a particular raid

Taxidermist, go and see the – get stuffed. Introduced in 1943

Twilights – the lighter, summer-weight knickers of a WAAF (as opposed to the blackouts, the winter-weight version)

Wank-pit or Wanker – a bed, presumably where masturbation takes place

You know what you can do – stick it up your arse

5 Overpaid, Over-sexed, Over Here – and Over the Top[1]

Legend has it (and legend is wrong) that the first GI to come ashore in wartime Britain was Private First Class Milburn H. Henke from Hutchison, Minnesota, who landed with the 34th US Infantry Division at Belfast.[2] His father was a naturalized German, but never mind, we were all very grateful for Uncle Sam's help.

The Yanks brought men, guns, ammunition and money, and there is no doubt that Operation Overlord

---

[1] All right – I'll come clean; I added the 'Over the Top' bit. The GIs themselves, of course, complained that they were 'underfed, underpaid, undersexed and under Eisenhower'.

[2] It would be interesting to find out what kind of slang impact the Americans of Eagle Squadron had on the RAF. They were volunteers who joined Britain months ahead of the official declaration of war by the United States in December 1941.

could not have worked without them. But they also brought their own racial baggage, their candy, their guns and their jeeps, and a gung-ho attitude that changed Britain forever. One woman, asked for her memories of the Second World War, said that she didn't remember the war at all, but she remembered the Americans. One of the first pieces of advice the US troops were given was 'Flies spread diseases. Keep yours buttoned!' But they didn't listen: VD was up by 70 per cent among American forces within six months of their arrival; 70,000 British women went home as GI brides in 1945 and thousands more had little diaper-clad[3] reminders of what today we call the 'special relationship'. They also upped the gear of swearing quite considerably.

It was not supposed to be like that. Before the war, the biggest American influence in Britain was via the cinema, to which vast numbers of Britons were addicted. A history of swearing in the United States follows much the same pattern as ours – obviously so, since the original thirteen colonies were British. As in Britain, it was assumed to be a class thing. So in 1889, an American clergyman wrote that swearing 'is the vice of the lower classes, of the drunken classes, of the mean and vicious souls who swear best when they are dirtiest and most un-manlike'.

In a military context, George Washington, commander of the Continental (i.e. American) Army in the

---

[3] Nappies have still, mercifully, not been usurped by the American translation.

War of Independence (1775–83) issued orders to his troops to avoid the profanity of cursing and swearing. The tough-guy image associated with the Frontier and the American West almost demanded bad language, although the 1880s 'horse's caboose' (arse), 'doggone' (goddamn), 'gee whiz' (Jesus) and 'son-of-a-gun' (son of a bitch) sound rather tame and decidedly quaint today.[4]

By the 1930s polite America was trying to maintain standards. In 1935 a woman was prosecuted for telling a policeman to mind his own goddamn business and the Hays Commission got to work to clean up the language and the behaviour of the big screen. Notoriously, the last line of *Gone with the Wind*, released in 1939, had Rhett Butler (Clark Gable) saying to Scarlett O'Hara (Vivien Leigh), 'Frankly, my dear, I don't give a damn.' The Hays people had wanted 'I don't really care' instead but either the producer, David O. Selznick, paid the massive fine involved or the law was changed at the last minute (the jury is still out on that one).

H. L. Mencken was concerned that the language of the Doughboys, as US soldiers were nicknamed since the Great War, had deteriorated. 'It is all based upon one or two four-letter words and their derivatives and there is little true profanity in it,' he said, optimistically. The *Infantry Journal* of 1943 went further:

---

[4] The recent, expletive-laden *Deadwood* western series, set in the mining town of the same name in the 1870s, is just about as wide of the mark on swearing as it is possible to be.

The Army does not officially condone profanity; unofficially it knows it can do little to stop it. The society of soldiers is not polite. It is a society of men, frequently unwashed, who have been dedicated to the rugged task of killing other men, and whose training has emphasised that a certain reversion to the primitive is not undesirable.

This idea is fascinating. The implication is that killing is a profane business and you cannot do the job properly without a little bad language. General George S. Patton of the Third Army held similar beliefs, as we shall see.

Punch summed up the situation perfectly in 1942:

> Dear old England's not the same,
> The dread invasion, well, it came.
> But no, it's not the beastly Hun,
> The god-damn Yankee army's come.

There was, perhaps, a certain irony here. The French had called the British the Goddamns since the fourteenth century because apparently we swore so much, but by 1942 the phrase was exclusively thought of as American.

So how bad was bad when it came to American Forces' slang? Although some of the Second World War terms in *The Slanguage of Sex* are debatable as to their country of origin, some are definitely from across the Pond.

The A–Z (actually B–Y) of US Swearing

Beard – female partner of a male homosexual who is there for acceptability's sake. Although this is US 1940s slang, it was very unlikely to be used in the visiting forces. Homosexuality was illegal, as it was in civilian life, and attitudes towards it differed accordingly

Bell – clitoris (as in 'ring my bell'). Black Second World War slang and an example of the racial divide the Americans imported during the war

Bitch – woman. In keeping with quite a bit of American

slang, its origin is prison-speak, especially among the black community

Cat's head cut open – female genitals. Cat was nineteenth-century American speak for a prostitute and a cathouse was a brothel

Cheesecake – erotic/pornographic pictures of women. Some of these were available in the 'girlie' magazines of the day (in the photographs, women had no genitals at all) and were occasionally painted by artistic GIs on the walls of captured houses and barns and, more permanently, on the fuselage of aircraft, e.g. the *Memphis Belle*, the first American bomber to complete twenty-five operational missions

Clap – venereal disease (especially gonorrhoea) although this was used in England as early as the sixteenth century

Dear John – a tragic letter from the girl back home telling her sweetheart it was all over. By 1945, however, it might already have acquired the meaning that the girl had given said sweetheart VD

Fag(got) – homosexual, especially of the passive variety

Fairy – homosexual

Girl – homosexual, especially of the cross-dressing variety

Good-time girl – prostitute (see Call girl in the General section of Chapter 4)

Honey-basket – shit container, an article handled by camp orderlies

Jersey City – breast (as in titty, a good example of cockney rhyming slang travelling 3,000 miles)

Marble Arch-style – intercourse, standing up and fully clothed. Even some prostitutes believed it was impossible to get pregnant that way

Nooky – sexual fumblings

Pansy – homosexual

Panty-waist – cissy, effeminate person. A more modern version might be 'big girl's blouse'

Punk – homosexual. This originally referred to a female prostitute which is presumably from where the term developed

Rubber – contraceptive. There was a rumour that the American variety had steel tips

Snowdrop – Military Policeman, recognizable by the white helmet. Not a crude term in itself, it was usually accompanied by the F-word (see Absolute bastards in General section of Chapter 4)

Spam basher – British girl who went out with a GI usually in exchange for nylons and candy

Tenderloin – prostitute

Trick – a prostitute's client; also 'John' as the most common name a man would use to introduce himself to a prostitute

Wall job – see Marble Arch-style, above

Yankee bag – see Spam basher, above

Hammer – I have put this one out of alphabetical order because it is technically Canadian. It means penis and comes from the weapon/tool metaphor we have seen before

Myth 4
We All Speak the Same Bad Language:
Pissed v. Pissed

One of the problems about language is that different words mean different things on either side of the Atlantic. Pissed is a classic case. In America, it means annoyed; in Britain, paralytic with drink.

The poet Louis MacNeice did his bit for propaganda when he wrote *The Short Guide for GIs* about to arrive in the UK. 'It isn't a good idea to say "bloody" in mixed company in Britain. It is one of their worst swear words. To say "I look like a bum" is offensive to their ears, for to the British this means that you are trying to look like your own backsides.'

There were all sorts of misunderstandings about 'rubbers' and 'erasers' and several of the milder GIs were rather taken aback to be told to keep their pecker up. 'Fanny' raised eyebrows and it was an ignorant landlady indeed who offered to 'knock up' their GI lodgers with a cup of tea. Americans stationed in Norfolk would try to photograph their latest 'cutie' in front of an innocent nautical sign that read 'Navigation on this Broad is free'.

Even clean language could be misconstrued. A civilian contributor to a live BBC wireless broadcast assured listeners that while he hadn't seen Eleanor Roosevelt himself (this referred to the visit of the President's wife in November 1942) he understood that 'her chief purpose in coming here is to have intercourse with the American troops'. Way to go, Eleanor!

'I'm twice as pissed!' (apologies to Bill Maudlin, the famous American wartime cartoonist)

What about the Yanks in action?

When General Anthony McAuliffe was asked by the Germans to surrender Bastogne in Belgium on 22 December 1944, his famous answer was 'Nuts!' As this is American for balls or bollocks, I suspect the Germans got the gist. All power to the General's grasp of history because it chimes with a similar remark from the French General Cambronne at the end of the battle of Waterloo. Called upon by the British to surrender the Old Guard, he yelled *'Merde!'* ('Shit!') – see note in Chapter 3.[5]

Just as the British had a 'forgotten army' in the Second World War – the men who surrendered at Singapore and spent the next three years building the Burma Railway – so the Americans had one in the Philippines in 1942:

> We're the battling bastards of Bataan;
> No mama, no papa, no Uncle Sam;
> No aunts, no uncles, no cousins, no nieces;
> No pills, no planes, no artillery pieces
> And nobody gives a damn.

The Americans were involved in D-Day, too, getting the rough edge of the German defences at Omaha Beach in particular. One of the generals on that beach was Norman 'Dutch' Cota. Dodging machine-gun bullets,

---

[5] Interestingly, polite society claimed that Cambronne actually said 'The Guard dies, but it does not surrender' – all very noble, but unlikely.

he came upon a group of soldiers trying to hide in a sand dune. 'Who are you people?' he asked. Sergeant Mike Rehan answered him: 'Sir, we're Rangers.' Cota was appalled. 'Godammit, if you're Rangers, get up there and clear the way.'

Donald Burgett of the 101st Airborne was content to swear to himself when a Luftwaffe plane screamed over-head, spraying the men on the ground: 'That dirty son of a bitch pilot.' The *Stars and Stripes* Forces newspaper gave sensible advice to Americans setting foot in France for the first time: 'Don't be surprised if a Frenchman steps up and kisses you. That doesn't mean he's queer. It means he's French and darn glad to see you.' P. H. B. Pritchard of No. 6 Commando, 1st Special Brigade, overheard a soldier who was less than enchanted, how-ever: 'When I left the States, I thought I was going to be a soldier, but here I am emptying p—s buckets. I guess the folks back home will call me chicken s—t!' And that was the nickname they gave him!

Our perception of the Second World War is wrong. The films get the uniforms right (more or less) and the haircuts (although it is usually too long for the chaps) but the language usually misses by a mile. In July 2001 a group of veterans were taken to a special pre-screening of the hit television series *Band of Brothers*. They enjoyed it and all agreed that everything was accurate, *except the bad language*: 'We didn't talk like that. We were mostly farm boys coming out of the Depression and we never used the f-word like that. And we never disrespected women by using bad language around them.'

Getting past the censor

There were 12,000 black soldiers in Britain by the summer of 1942 and their very unusualness made them a hit with local girls. The non-white population of Britain was tiny in wartime. Chief Superintendent Ted Greeno of the Metropolitan Police took people on tours of London, including to the East End's Cable Street 'where the negroes walked'. White girls dancing with black men led to punch-ups, almost always from other GIs. Blacks could not join the elite outfits like the Marine Corps or the Air Corps.

There was trouble in Birmingham where white GIs kicked black ones off the 'sidewalk' calling them 'black trash'. One soldier in the 11th Armoured Division told a Chippenham woman in a matter-of-fact tone, 'Ma'am, we shoot niggers where I come from.'

At home, the Ku Klux Klan was still attracting thousands and several states operated the 'Jim Crow' laws which kept blacks segregated and politically powerless. To many of the old South's 'rednecks', Lincoln's Emancipation Proclamation of 1863 was just a serving suggestion.

The Cocksucker Proxy

General George C. Patton earned a reputation in the Second World War like no other. His speech to the 6th Armoured Division in 1944 has gone down in history for its profanity. For those of you who like analysis, there are:

> 11 Hells
> 10 Shits
> 6 Sons of Bitches
> 4 Goddamneds
> 3 Fucks
> 3 Pisses
> 2 Bastards
> 1 Cocksucker
> and
> 1 Asshole

That's a total of forty-one swear words, which actually isn't very many in the hundreds he used, but they are the ones we remember. He knew his men hated what they called 'chicken shit drilling'. There was always a risk that 'a German son-of-an-asshole-bitch' was going to sneak up behind them and beat them to 'death with a sockful of shit'. The heroic stuff that journalists wrote about 'is pure horseshit' and they were all 'bilious bastards, especially if they wrote for the *Saturday Evening Post*'. Such men knew less about fighting than 'they know about fucking'. The Army's job was to eliminate the 'Goddamned cowards' and the 'Goddamned Germans' and then turn on the 'purple pissing Japs' – preferably before the 'Goddamned Marines' got all the credit.

As for Patton, he was off to Berlin to shoot that 'paper-hanging[6] son of a bitch Hitler', adding, 'We're going to murder those lousy Hun cocksuckers by the bushel-fucking basket.' What is most revealing is his audience's reaction; they loved it, cheering and whooping, which probably drove him on to be even more over the top. Patton's nephew remembered the General explaining why he had said what he did: 'You can't run an army without profanity; and it has to be eloquent profanity. An army without profanity couldn't fight its way out of a piss-soaked paper bag.'

And who told them this? . . . 'a Son-of-a-Goddamned-Bitch named Georgie Patton!'

And as he said at the end of his oration, 'Ahh, I feel much better!'

I think his audience did too.

---

[6] The common perception was that this was Hitler's job before he became Führer. This dates from the time when, before the Great War, he had failed to get into the Vienna School of Art and painted postcards of street scenes to survive.

WALOBA (What A Load Of Bloody Acronyms)

When it comes to wartime acronyms, most people think that the naughtiest the British had was ITMA – the radio show *It's That Man Again* starring Tommy Handley. Actually, that's not quite true. We also had:

FUMTU – Fucked Up More Than Usual

IMFU – Imperial Military Fuck Up (a mistake on a colossal scale). Technically, anything after 1877 was Imperial because that was when Queen Victoria took the title Empress

MFT – Military Fuck Up (on a minor or average scale)

NABU – Non-Adjustable Balls Up

SABU – Self-Adjusting Balls Up (so, presumably, not so bad)

TABU – Typical Army Balls Up

TCCFU – Typical Coastal Command Fuck Up (as said by Coastal Command themselves)

The Americans were far more imaginative and invented the following (in chronological order):

SUSFU – Situation Usual, Still Fucked Up (*American Notes and Queries*, September 1941).

Please note that this one predates American entry into the war by four months!

SNAFU – Situation Normal, All Fucked Up (*US Marine Corps*, 16 January 1942)

FUBAR – Fucked Up Beyond All Recognition (*Yank Army Weekly*, 7 January 1944)

TARFU – Things Are Really Fucked Up (from the short film *Three Brothers*, 1944, which featured two Army privates – Snafu and Fubar – and Seaman Tarfu

The acronyms themselves were harmless of course, so *Time* magazine felt perfectly justified in writing for the folks back home: 'citizens knew that gasoline rationing and rubber requisitions were snafu'.

6 'What Did You Swear in the War, Daddy?'

'No swearing. There may be gentlemen about.'
– NOTICE IN AN ALL-FEMALE MUNITIONS FACTORY, 1944

VE (Victory in Europe) Day took place on 8 May 1945.

VJ (Victory in Japan) Day followed soon after on 15 August.

The Allies had closed in on Berlin from east and west, driving the Wehrmacht into pockets where they surrendered in droves. Before the Cold War and the threat from communist Russia, many people in Britain regarded the 'Ruskies' as bosom pals. Don't believe me? Try singing this to the tune of 'The Lincolnshire Poacher' (hint – the 'proper' song starts 'When I was bound apprentice in famous Lincolnshire . . .'):

That Hitler's armies can't be beat is just a load of cock,
For Marshal Timoshenko's boys are pissing through

> von Bock,
> The Führer makes the bloomers and his marshals
>   take the rap;
> Meanwhile Joe[7] smokes a pipe and wears a
>   taxi-driver's cap.

In the Far East, the Fourteenth Army had retaken Burma and the Americans were island-hopping, retaking the Pacific from the Japanese. In one of the most controversial decisions of the war, President Harry S. Truman ordered the atomic bombing of Hiroshima and Nagasaki which forced the Japanese to surrender.

So the war was over, but the swearing wasn't. Let me give you two examples from my own experience. I was the tail-end of the post-war bulge. I was born in 1949 and by 1953 was to be found running up the road trying to catch my older cousin who could run faster than me, yelling, 'Bugger! Bugger! Bugger!' at her. I had no idea what the word meant but it sounded good and made me feel better. Apparently I'd picked the word up from my uncle (my cousin's father) so it was actually payback time.

Years later, a grim-faced headmaster stood in front of the 600+ boys who attended my senior school somewhere in England and told us he was horrified to have found, on the wall of one of the toilet cubicles (and I quote), 'The word C-U-N-T with an illustration!' He

---

7 Semyon Timoshenko was a Bolshevik general. Fedor von Bock was a Nazi general who was dismissed by Hitler when he failed to take Moscow. Joe is Josef Stalin, the Soviet dictator.

then proceeded to tell us that in all his years in the Army (he served during the war and was Mentioned in Despatches) he had never come across anything like it. Even as a fourteen-year-old, I wondered what kind of Army he had been in. Sally, perhaps?

In June 1941 there were 2.25 million men in the British Army; 395,000 in the Navy and 662,000 in the RAF. The complete female tally for all three services was over 100,000. An estimated 3.5 million men had served in the Armed Forces over the six years of conflict and thousands of others wore uniforms of all sorts – the police, the fire service, ARP wardens, fire-watchers, coastguards – and all of those had wives, sisters, mothers, girlfriends and female next-door neighbours whose lives had been changed forever by the war. Women had worked in munitions and had driven tractors in the Land Army. They had flown Spitfires from factories to airbases. They had handled radios and radar equipment for the Navy and the RAF. They had broken codes at Bletchley Park. In short, they had done their bit. And there were thousands of prostitutes who did their bit too – the GIs called them Piccadilly Commandoes or Hyde Park Rangers, almost as if they were extensions of the Armed Forces.

An American commentator, Bernard DeVoto, has this to say about the post-war situation in the United States: 'Military life made most of the monosyllables automatic in the conversation of the soldiers and sailors whom millions of women knew.' But there was more to it than that. 'Fuck', for example, came to signify 'frankness, sophistication, liberalism, companiona-bility and even smartness' among a very great many educated and well-to-do metropolitan women. There is no doubt that after the war, all things American caught on in Britain. It was only the 'age of austerity', perhaps, that prevented it from happening sooner. Televisions and freezers and cars were beyond the wildest dreams of people still struggling with rationing, and that did not end until 1953. But ideas – and language – were free and we can assume that a certain amount of the rude variety, already brought over by the GIs, never went away and that new variants kept appearing.

Soon after 1945, women from all walks of life began to do all the things they hadn't before the war – they smoked in public, they went alone to pubs, they asked men to dance in dance halls. And, like the men, they started to swear.

So did their children. The generation brought up during the war has been called the most delinquent in history. These kids were deprived in many cases of father figures because of conscription and battlefield casualties. They were denied regular education, espe-cially in cities, because the Blitz made their schools holes in the ground and many of their role-model male teachers were elsewhere. City children became feral tearaways. They picked up street language from their parents and they passed it on to the next gen-eration, embellishing a little bit as they went just because they could. So, a 'real East Ender', born in Southwark in 1938 and living in East Ham between

1940 and 1952, heard 'Fuck! Sod! Sod Off! Arseholes! and Bugger It!' every day of his life; he thought nothing of it.

Because lads like him were evacuated to the country (although it is true that most of them drifted back as soon as they could, missing the raucous life of the cities) they took their swearing to the slightly more genteel rural areas where the kids there were only too eager to pick it up.

From Here to Profanity

Remember that (in those days) naughty scene in the film *From Here to Eternity* where Burt Lancaster rolls around in the surf with Deborah Kerr? (What would the King of Siam say?) The film was based on the book of the same name by James Jones, written in 1951. It tells of a love story at the time of the Japanese attack on Pearl Harbor ten years earlier and Jones used the word 'fuck' 240 times and the word 'shit' 85. Nervous editors made him reduce the numbers, respectively, to 108 and 50.

In 1948 Norman Mailer had tried to get around the problem in *The Naked and the Dead* by using 'fug' instead of 'fuck'. This didn't really fool anybody, least of all the acerbic actress Tallulah Bankhead, who, when introduced to Mailer, said, 'So you're the young man who can't spell fuck.'

Swearing on Celluloid

In one of the most heart-rending scenes in *The Cruel Sea*, Jack Hawkins (who else?) has tears trickling down his cheeks because he has just ordered his ship to ignore men in the sea, drowning and desperate for help. 'It's the bloody war,' he says, by way of explanation.

Five years after it was all over, Dirk Bogarde played a young tearaway who shot an endearing copper of the old school, played by Jack Warner, in *The Blue Lamp*. Nobody in the audience minded very much when one of the policemen said, 'We're on to the bastard who shot George Dixon.'

Anderson shelters sprang up like mushrooms on the home front. They were corrugated iron air-raid shelters and liable to flood. The heroes of the home front – firemen, ambulancemen and police – spent a lot of time pumping these out. Bizarrely, some of these men came in for 'stick' because they weren't in the Armed Forces. One recalled, 'Not being thin-skinned the candid remarks so often heard about three-pounds-a-week men doing bugger all for their money didn't worry me at all.'

Although defeatism was officially a crime under Churchill's government, it didn't stop soldiers whinging to civilians. Basil Dean, the director of ENSA (Entertainments National Service Association), remembered sitting in a pub, 'listening to the seething soldiery (yes, that is the only adjective to use) expressing blasphemous resentment at what had happened to them'. Unfortunately, Dean doesn't tell us exactly what they said!

Newspapers tentatively led the way on the swearing front. The Great Australian Adjective became a banner headline in the *Daily Mirror* in the context of the successful evacuation from Dunkirk in May 1940 (338,226 men were brought home by the 'little ships' of the south coast) – 'Bloody Marvellous!' (see Chapter 2).

Churchill could, no doubt, swear for England, although his official speeches avoided that. In the famous 'we shall fight' oration, he is reputed to have broken off to deliver an aside (not reported in Hansard) 'and beat the bastards about the head with bottles; it's all we've got'.

The panic caused by the Blitz probably sent swearing off the scale. As the Surrey Docks blazed along the Thames in the autumn of 1940, a fire officer sent a message to his chief: 'Send all the bloody pumps you've got; the whole bloody world's on fire.' In May of the following year, rescue workers in Bermondsey were asked to nominate people for decorations recognizing their bravery: 'Medals? We don't want no fucking medals. The whole fucking borough deserves a fucking medal.'[8]

An American journalist, from a country not yet at

---

[8] I have substituted the 'f' word from what I know of Bermondsey! In the original (*Your Obedient Servant*, Sir Harold Scott, Commissioner of the Metropolitan Police) there is the dreaded straight line.

war in 1940, made a collection of overheard conversations in the London Underground shelters and they illustrate the euphemisms of the day:

'We didn't ask for the blinking war, did we?'

'No wonder Germany's not fed up – they've *got* some blinking air raid shelters!'

'Bloody LCC red tape!'

It's interesting that the only real expletive is reserved for the London County Council!

As London's Guildhall burned at the end of December 1940, one eyewitness likened the efforts of the firemen to 'little boys peeing on an enormous bonfire'. Incidentally, there was revenge of a kind in the spring of 1945 when Churchill and various members of the Allied high command peed into the Rhine as the British and Americans thundered east in the race for Berlin. Members of the Press Corps were asked not to film that particular incident.

The only part of the UK occupied by German forces were the Channel Islands. Here the civilians faced the same problem as anybody under the boots of the Third Reich – fight, flee or come to an arrangement with the conquerors. Girls on Guernsey, who had chosen the last option, were called 'Jerrybags'.

The dislocation caused by the war led to some colourful interchanges of language. It was not only kids who were evacuated to the country. Land girls had to get used to this, too. Rachel Knappett found herself on a farm in Lancashire where a labourer asked her politely to move: 'Cum art road, yer gawpin' bugger.'

She became the 'bloody wench' to the locals and realized over time that both these words were terms of endearment.

A glimpse of the criminal classes at home gives us perhaps the clearest and least inhibited use of bad language. Because of the ongoing paranoia of the government, terrified of a Fifth Column of spies operating in the country, honest citizens often came under a cloud of suspicion and some of them were imprisoned. In April 1944 a small trader wrote in exasperation to the Chancellor of the Exchequer, Sir John Anderson:

> The government has governed my business until
> I do not know who the bloody hell owns it. I am
> suspected, inspected, examined, informed, required
> and commanded so that I do not know who the hell
> I am and where I am or why I am here at all . . .
> The only reason I am clinging to life at all is to see
> what the Bloody Hell is going to happen next.

The air-raid shelters caused problems in all sorts of ways – sanitary problems, overcrowding, illicit sex. They also caused swearing. In October 1940, 200 protesters marched on Stepney ARP Control Centre and attacked wardens and the police. 'Come on!' the twenty-one-year-old girl leading them shouted. 'Let's get the yellow bastards!' At a shelter in Tilbury three months later, outsiders trying to get in caused a punch-up. 'We want bloody Hitler here to deal with you bastards!'

When the police arrived to restore order, Mrs Agnes Squibbs, a respectable local mother of several, yelled, 'Let's get them bastards!' and promptly set about as many of the Met as she could reach.

The police, as always, took the brunt of the public's fear and frustration. DS Layfield and his men found two deserters who were at home with their mother in Balham in the autumn of 1942. While one of the men raised a hammer, his kid brother grabbed a bottle: 'I will split your fucking head open.' Mum didn't hold back either. 'You are two of Churchill's bastards. You are like the rest of your Home Secretary's clique of conchies! When Germany wins, you will all be out of a job.' The boys were returned to the Army and their mother was fined £2.

Gradually, things returned to normal. Rationing, it is true, had eight more years to run after the war and everywhere there were holes in the ground where houses and shops once stood. In a bizarre twist, Winston Churchill, who had come to personify the bulldog resilience of the British throughout the war, lost the election of 1945 and Clement Attlee's Labour government ushered in the Welfare State.

Men came home from all parts of the world, handed in their rifles and hung up their kitbags. In the country, tin hats became containers for chicken-feed and thousands of useless gasmasks appeared in junk-shop windows. The true horror of the war was brought home to a disbelieving public who read the details of the Holocaust and there was a grim satisfaction when leading Nazis were hanged by Albert Pierrepoint, Britain's own executioner, after Nuremberg.

The world, of course, turned and other wars followed. The former ally, the Soviet Union, turned out to be yet another threat as East and West squared up to each other and Germany was split into communist versus democrat. Some of the men on both sides of the Atlantic who had served in the Second World War soon found themselves together again, fighting the communists in Korea. Douglas MacArthur was there too.

In America, in a way, it was business as usual. When asked why he had fired General MacArthur in April 1951, President Harry S. Truman said, 'I fired him because he wouldn't respect the authority of the President . . . I didn't fire him because he was a dumb son-of-a-bitch, although he was.'

Had a way with words, did Harry S; but actually, I'm cheating here. This was not officially quoted until 1973, by which time anything spoken during the Second World War seemed decidedly tame.

The casualty rates of the Second World War are staggering, especially since they involved civilians on an unprecedented scale. I have taken a tongue-in-cheek, sideways look at this period in this book, but the humour in it is gallows humour – used to disguise a time of appalling atrocities and unrelieved misery. By 1945 over fifty-five million people had died.

What happened to the key people we have met along slang's highway? The poets of the Great War, Robert Graves and Siegfried Sassoon lasted long after most of their contemporaries. Sassoon – 'Mad Jack' to a generation – died in 1967; Graves, an elder statesman of literature, in 1985. The political leaders of the Third Reich, sent up mercilessly in the various ditties of the war, all came to sticky ends. Rumours persisted that Hitler lived on, in various countries and various disguises, for years, but the reality is, as we have seen, that he committed suicide in Berlin in 1945. Josef Goebbels, his Propaganda Minister, followed suit soon after by swallowing poison. Himmler died that way too, already under guard by the British, and Goering, defiant to the last, cheated the hangman by biting on a cyanide capsule in Nuremberg prison. Benito Mussolini, the Italian dictator, was shot by his own people in April 1945, his body kicked and spat on by disillusioned Italians. Of the dictators, only 'Uncle Joe' Stalin survived, dying in suspicious circumstances in 1953, guilty of nearly as many crimes as Hitler.

Neville Chamberlain, the Prime Minister who gave way to Churchill, died of cancer in 1940 and Churchill himself, the man of the millennium, followed him in 1965, the cranes of London's dockland bowing in respect as his coffin was towed upriver.

The literary giants who contributed to the wittiest use of slang lived on for a long time. Noël Coward died in 1973, two years after A. P. Herbert. J. B. Priestley, the grand old man of a forgotten England, lasted until 1984. And Eric Partridge, to whom any writer on slang owes a great deal, died in 1979.

Of soldiers, sailors and airmen, Guy Gibson of

Dambusters fame was killed in a bombing mission in 1944; 'Old Blood and Guts' George Patton died the following year. Dwight Eisenhower, the Supreme Commander of Overlord, passed away in 1969, but not before he had become President of the United States. His comrade, Bernard Montgomery, never exactly a friend of his, died in 1976.

One of the few names forever associated with the war, the Forces sweetheart Vera Lynn, is still with us and it is perhaps fitting to leave the last word to her (in a paraphrased way, of course). The haunting 'White Cliffs of Dover' should, possibly, have different lyrics:

> There'll be blue words over
> The White Cliffs of Dover – tomorrow,
>   just you wait and see.
> There'll be love and laughter,
> And swearing ever after,
> Tomorrow – when the world is free.